9 - 5 IS FOR DUMMIES

Tips On How To Get Out Of Your Hell Job

Contents

INTRODUCTION

Imagine for a moment, the possibility of quitting that job that is reducing your quality of life in the next ten minutes. Well, possibly that may be an imprudent thing to do, but if you have savings and reserve capital to be able to live for a few months, maybe doing just that is the best thing to do.

Making an income from home is a dream of many people. The idea of waking at a civilized hour and maintaining a strict regimen of natural work flow, having lunch with friends and going out late at night can be a fun lifestyle. It certainly beats the 9 to 5 rat race.

But the question is how to get out of your day Job. Fortunately it is not as difficult as one may suppose. There are several ways one can quit his or her job without hassles.

In this book are proven ways one can quit his or her job as well as pointers to know when to quit. enjoy it!

GET OUT OF YOUR COMFORT ZONE

Greatness exists outside people's comfort zone. Those who attain the greatest of achievements, do so because they put themselves on the line. They take the action that many others shy away from. Doing what the masses will not is what separates the successful from the rest of the group. Unfortunately, society seems to ignore this fact while promoting the exact opposite. We are all told how it is best to take the safe route. It is important to get ourselves a good education which will lead to a good job with benefits. This will result in us being secure and happy. Of course, we all know how this sentiment was proven untrue over the past 20-30 years.

Developing the habit of stretching our comfort zones is one of the most important things that we can do to ensure our self growth. Too many people have the goal of being comfortable their entire lives. They try to set everything up so that the surprises are kept to a minimum. Remaining in the same job is a common way to stay in the circle of comfort.

While the person wants more, the fact that he or she knows what to expect is more desirable. The fear associated with stepping out is simply too great. Naturally, most cannot admit that it is fear holding them back. Rather, they rationalize it by claiming that they are being responsible, smart, or prudent.

Typically, people avoid doing something different for fear of looking bad. If they cannot be successful at the activity the first time, they will not try it. Of course, this is a philosophy that will paralyze people. Almost nobody is good at an activity the first time they do it. Most things take practice. Over time, we develop some form of competence if we work at something. Yet, the highest percentage of people will refuse to do this because of this fear.

I am sure that you have met people who live their lives in exactly the same manner. Whenever they go out to eat, they attend the same restaurants. To make matters

worse, they order the same thing off the menu each time. They believe in the concept of sticking with what is 'tried and true'. Ultimately, their lives tend to be boring.

Each week resembles the previous one. The same television programs are watched. They leave for and arrive home from work at exactly the same time. Of course, the route never wavers.

If you desire more out of life, begin by getting out of your comfort zone. At first, it can be done in a simple but effective way. Perhaps go see a movie that you typically would not see. Try a different restaurant, especially one that serves food from a different culture. Alter your routine in any way that you can imagine. This begins to breed the habit of doing things a bit differently. While not instilling fear, for many even this stage is extremely difficult.

The next part of the process will really scare you. Go do something that puts you at risk. By this we are not necessarily referring to bodily harm.

We are alluding to those things that you believe will make you look foolish. A great way to do this is to go up and talk to a total stranger. Do this the next time you are at a party. A wonderful ice breaker is to say 'Hi, I am Juliana'. If this idea terrifies you, it is exactly what you need to do.

Also, decide to do an activity that you have never done before. Do not worry about looking foolish. That is part of the journey. Ultimately, you might just find something else that you truly enjoy. Finally, if you want to blast out of your comfort zone, do some public speaking. Surveys found that people fear this more than death. Are you one that fits into this category? If so, join Toastmasters or take a public speaking course at a local community college. It will do wonders for instilling confidence within you.

Life is not meant to be lived in a box. An unexamined life is not worth living. Do you simply repeat each day without any thought of change. To have comfort as a goal in life leads to a miserable existence. The forces of nature cannot be harnessed.

Regardless of how much we try to avoid uncomfortable situations, life has a way of serving them up to us anyway. Why not take the initiative and seek out those uncomfortable situations? It is always better to do things on our terms. Also, it is much easier to emotionally deal with something if we are the ones seeking it out. As we develop this habit, we are better able to handle the unexpected that life tends to offer.

WHEN A GOOD JOB GOES BAD: KNOW WHAT TO DO

Every job starts out from a positive perspective, whether that job represents hope, renewal, self-actualization, desperately needed income, or even a second chance. That initial momentum eventually shifts as a person settles into their job and becomes familiar with the requirements and expectations of the job, along with the working conditions, ethical standards, norms, and overall culture of the organization.

Throughout the process of becoming acclimated to a new job and working environment there will likely be unexpected situations and circumstances that come up, and that is when the reality of the job begins to settle in. Over the course of any typical job, there may be disputes or disagreements. There may be some colleagues who are easier to work with than others. For example, one person can be challenging to work with while another shows appreciation.

Rarely is any job perfect and everyone has a particular level of what can be tolerated, whether or not it is consciously recognized and acknowledged. On occasion a new job, one that felt good at the beginning, can seem to go bad and if it does - it may seem to be beyond your control. But you always have a choice as to how you respond, whether you take flight, fight, or do nothing. The outcome of your action depends upon whether it was done from an emotional or rational perspective.

Triggering Events

Working with a wide variety of personalities, changing job requirements, demanding expectations, or stressful working conditions can challenge the established internalized threshold for what can be accepted. For many people it is a balancing act. As an example, the working conditions may be poor but the pay is good so the tradeoff is acceptable. Or the pay is low but the manager is especially engaging and enjoyable to work with most days.

But that tolerance level may have to be adjusted, especially when an issue arises that pushes past it. That triggering event raises awareness of the internalized threshold level and now something must be done to address it.

Often a triggering event feels like the last straw, especially when a person has continued to put up with circumstances at work and a line was drawn - and someone or something has now crossed it. The threshold is now consciously recognized and must be dealt with internally (emotional response) or externally (some form of confrontation or retaliation). Dealing with triggering events externally first can make an uncomfortable situation better or more likely, worse. That's why it should be a strategic response, which is tough to do when emotions are running high and it feels as if it is no longer possible to tolerate or put up with current conditions.

Fight or Flight Reactions

A triggering event may seem like it has come out of the blue; however, a job may have actually been going bad for quite some time and it isn't until there is a culmination of events that a crisis point is reached, which is the time when it gets your attention.

Then the situation or triggering event seems to demand some form of resolution from you. Personality clashes at work are usually the most difficult to resolve.

A third party or the use of allies to intervene may be needed, and if you truly develop a dislike for someone a decision must be made as to whether or not you can work with them for the sake of the job, or even your future career.

The initial reaction for many people is to fight, by pushing back or speaking up. It could also manifest in the form of performance declining and/or withdrawing from others at work. One choice that never usually works well is retaliation, as it will only continue to maintain negative emotions.

When a job seems to become unbearable it can be hard to get back to the initial feeling of excitement that was experienced when beginning this job.

That is when a second option of finding new employment, quitting, or taking flight may seem like the best response. Both fight and flight are reactive, often emotional responses, and do not usually result in the best use of judgement. A better option is to wait and avoid reacting or making decisions until you can switch from being emotional to thinking in a more rational manner.

Do Nothing When a Good Job Goes Bad

When a job reaches a crisis point, or something has occurred that pushes past the internalized threshold or comfort level, there are usually strong emotions involved. It is natural to then ask questions, in an attempt to pinpoint a precise reason why the events occurred or why this happened to you. In other words, you may want to get to the bottom of it, figure it out, and perhaps blame someone. If this mental attitude continues for any length of time it can lead to self-doubt, anger, frustration, and other strong, negative emotions. But somehow you have to find a way to address those emotions before you fight or take flight, otherwise you may make a decision that you later wish you hadn't or eventually come to regret.

It can be helpful to switch to a rational mode, which can take time and practice, and consider the bigger picture. What are your career plans and goals? What are the benefits of staying or leaving? Do you have still more to learn from this job? Are there new skills you can still acquire? Then as you think rationally you can become more productive with your response. For example, what can you do now to make the situation more tolerable?

If this involved another employee, can you make the first step to repair the situation or relationship? Is there another team or department you can transfer to if the personality clash continues? Even a temporary change in the situation can help you reset how you feel about the job. Everyone understands that no job is going to be perfect. There will be an ebb and flow of ups and down times, disputes and disagreements, and circumstances that may be less than desirable.

When your personal threshold has been crossed the best course of action is to take a mental time out rather than fighting or taking flight. Engage yourself in reflection and emotional assessment.

Seek out friends you trust and have your best interest at heart, who can help you work through these situations. More importantly, conduct a career self-assessment and consider the role of this job in your career plans. The best question you can ask yourself is this: would another job be that much better?

When a good job goes bad you may have to leave but before you do, make sure you've made the change from a mindset of being proactive with your career rather than reactive and emotional. You are always in charge of your responses and your career.

KNOW WHEN IT'S TIME TO QUIT YOUR JOB

Quitting your job when things turn out bad for you is not a sign of weakness. Rather, it is a very smart thing to do. Because of the so-called job security, many workers even with these clear warning signals at times seem unable to decide to quit. Enduring a bad working situation is neither in your best interest nor even in the best interest of your company. Picking up the courage to quit if these warning signals become very obvious is not only good for your health and wellbeing, it benefits your company as well.

How do you personally know it's time to leave a job? What specifically can you point to at a time in your life when you've quit a job? Maybe even now you're in that place: dreading waking up on Monday, dreading the mundane tasks of doing work you're not passionate about.

Will you take your career into your own hands and make that tough decision to leave a job you don't want to be working anymore?

Here are ways to know when it's time to quit your job.

When your integrity and ethics are intact, but your innovation and drive are not.

You're a good person. You try to make sure you've dotted the "I's" and crossed the "t's". You work until two zeros follow the 5, and do the basics of your job as detailed from your manager. But that's where the quality in your work ethic ends. You've zoned out from your creativity.

You've given up on fresh, new ideas to get things done on the job. Not only that, you don't even give much effort into the new ideas your company has initiated. You care enough to not get fired, but that's about it. While others seem to go the extra mile, you feel pretty content hanging back while others pass you by.

When you dread Sundays because they lead to Mondays.

Weekends have a funny feeling when you hate your job. At the end of the day Friday, you're pumped. You've got 48 hours ahead of you to live your life the way you want. But Sunday comes fast, and before you've had the chance to soak up life, you're stuck in the drudgery of the "paycheck cycle". This is where your job has become nothing but a paycheck. You live for the weekend, you work for the paycheck. You hate Sundays, because all they do is lead to Mondays. It's like you're 16 years old again, and the weekends are awesome, but you'd rather get your wisdom teeth cut out than go to Monday morning's Algebra class.

When you spend your days at work daydreaming about your partner.

You have a passion. You have a partner. You have something there, somewhere deep inside, that gives you exuberant joy. It's not that this passion consumes you, but when you hate your life 40-50 hours a week, retreating mentally to a place you love is pretty easy.

Your partner is begging for your attention, the kind you barely give to your job. If this passion begins to steal away time at your job when you should be focused on work, that can be dangerous. It's important that you find time away from work to spend energy towards those interests. That quality time may lead to financial benefits down the line, or if nothing else, intense enjoyment.

When faking it is harder than ever.

You go to the meetings and throw out half-baked ideas on increasing sales. You ramble through conversations with co-workers about new products or new company initiatives. You see your boss, or his boss, or the boss of his boss, and masquerade enthusiasm like an Oscar winning actor. All the while, you're dying inside. You're wearing the mask as long as you can to make it to the end of the day where, for a few hours of downtime and sleep, you can remove it. Faking it is hard.

When you begin thinking more negatively about your company and its leadership.

It's not that the management at your company is bad, it's just that you simply don't care. And the longer you don't care, the more disdain you have for those that do. This happens especially when you've been with a company who doesn't value you or your opinion. If you work for a place where the management clearly has no interest in helping you get promoted or develop yourself, it's probably time to get out. Good management/leadership is evident when there is a true desire by those in charge to see those under them grow, develop, excel, and move up.

When your work is no longer valued by management.

You cannot possibly prove your continued employment when your employers no longer value your work. When management no longer values your work or even feels your presence, arrange to quit unless you want to top the list of those next on the firing line.

When your attitude at home matches your attitude at work.

This is the unfortunate part of hating your job. If your sour attitude about your work comes home with you, it will negatively affect your family. It will affect your spouse and your kids, and turn what should be your oasis away from work into a never-ending nightmare for you and your family. If you despise work so much that you cannot let that hatred go when you're home away from work, you need to get out. Fast!

When you have become disagreeable with corporate governance and culture.

Every business has its own corporate culture and governance style. As an employee, when you become completely disagreeable with this culture, it is time to quit.

When your job search is for "anything other than what you're doing".

The easiest thing to do when you hate your job is to start job searching. Not career searching... job searching. If you hate your job bad enough and long enough, then you'll be willing to look for anything that is not your job to go and do for money.

This doesn't do anyone any good, because if you leave a job you hate for another job you know you won't love, then you've extended your occupational depression into a new work environment with new management and new co-workers. It may feel good temporarily, but if your actual job doesn't bring you any satisfaction, you'll be back at square one. Even if you enjoy the people you work for and work with, the work itself will keep you from feeling happy.

When your career path has a dead end.

So many people stay at a job thinking their loyalty will earn them a promotion. In 2016, this couldn't be farther from the truth. Companies are no more loyal to you than you are to them. Everyone has to make that decision for themselves when their time is up for waiting out a promotion. If you've had at least two different opportunities and still weren't given a chance, it may be time to look elsewhere. Life is too short to spend time in a job where you're career path is a dead end.

When you're nervous about what your tombstone will say.

This could apply to an obituary as well. If you are scared of what your tombstone may say about you and your career, change. Think about what you would want an obit our tombstone to say about you when you're gone. "Here lies so and so who spent 50 years at so and so company as a mid-level manager." Now don't get me wrong. Being at one place that long even as just a mid-level manager may truly be a dream for some people. Essentially this is the rule of no regrets. Think about yourself at age 80. What do you want to look back on your life as having done? What kind of impact do you want to have made on others? Don't make this as much about the tombstone though. Consider the word "legacy". What will yours be?

When you are a victim of verbal abuse and other harassment.

No decent worker should ever accept verbal abuse or any other form of harassment in any employment. If you are being systematically abused or harassed sexually or otherwise, it is time to quit.

When you are no longer motivated to continue working.

There may come a time when you experience complete loss of enthusiasm to continue in your job. That it itself is a very clear signal that it is time to move on.

When you have become extremely disagreeable with your co-workers.

When you become extremely disagreeable with your co-workers, you have become a nuisance to yourself and everyone else. Don't wait to get fired. Just quit on your own volition.

When you have become stagnated in your current rank.

Stagnation brings about low morale and low drive to continue to work. Do not continue to endure it, just quit. That is best for you.

IDENTIFYING A BAD WORK ENVIRONMENT

As an employee, you are to identify a bad work experience early on before you are stuck there for years. If you are a manager it is good to review these three areas so you can spot these signs in your own groups and improve your teams.

For both employees and employers, it is good to know the major causes of dissatisfaction at work.

Keep in mind no company is 100% perfect and almost everyone will be able to connect with one or two of these workplace ailments, however if you see more than a few of these problems in your job then it may be time to consider that your company is not a happy place to work and could use some improvement.

Causes:

1. Your company - Is the entire company dysfunctional and a bad place to work?

Many companies create a work environment that makes being there eight hours a day (or more in many cases) an undignified experience. This could be the actual physical environment or this could mean the people in the company from the executive management team all the way down seem to be filled with jerks and shady characters.

• Employees fight against each other

The atmosphere of some companies feel like a dystopian wasteland where the motto is everyone for themselves. It is difficult to get help from other employees and departments, or even worse they actively try to sabotage your projects to make you look bad. This makes for a very stressful environment. Employees who get along with each other, help each other, and act like a supportive team generally function like one as well.

• No one gets promoted

Are you waiting for your manager to die so that you have a chance at promotion? Some companies are just not built to allow regular promotions. Maybe there is little growth or the bridge between job titles is too great. In these cases management needs to make up for the lack of real promotions with increased salary and additional numbers behind your job title. Even if there is no direct path from flight attendant to pilot, there should be a clear path to flight attendant level II and senior flight attendant. The company must provide a chance for growth, increased skills, learning programs, and regular salary increases above inflation adjustments.

• Responsibilities are increased without the corresponding increase in authority

If your company is expecting you to perform ever increasing tasks and lead projects and programs there needs to be a publicly known increase in authority that gives you the ability to accomplish these tasks. This should be done in the form of a new job title or a public announcement stating you are in charge of certain aspects of a program. This allows people to know that you are not just being nosey and bossy, but are doing your job.

• The skilled are not promoted

Often managers and entire companies reward friends or those who are most visible in the company over the most skilled and reasonable person for the job. This could be due to nepotism or it could be due to the skilled person being the only one who can perform a certain job and promoting them would move them away from the current job.

• High turnover rate

Constant reorganization is tough on employees rather it is caused by layoffs, firings, or a lack of loyalty toward the company or employees. It constantly changes work requirements, causes a loss of friends and security, and removes experts who are most knowledgeable about their roles. High turnover rate is both a sign and a cause of a bad workplace.

• No respect for employees

Employees are treated like property with no interest in their needs. They are never asked for their opinion, and never kept up to date on company direction. They are given no privacy, no independence, and are without the tools they need to perform at their best. Finally they are used up and spit out once they are no longer of value.

• Appearance more important than results

Companies often choose to measure work hours, meeting attendance, or the appearance that work is being done even if creating that appearance takes away from actual productivity.

These things often correspond with results, but it is the actual progress that matters in the end and results are what need to be counted. Sometimes a unique and unstructured workplace can birth the greatest creativity. Companies need to be mindful that one size does not fit all.

• No time off

Vacation is made available and advertised on job descriptions but cannot be used since everyone is too busy or taking vacation is frowned upon and seen as being lazy. Vacation accumulates and is lost. Employees lose their personal life and become burnt out.

• Payment is late or skipped

Company is not fiscally solvent enough or responsible enough to pay employees what was promised. Checks are late or missing. If this happens once due to some mistake it may be forgivable. If it happens often then the company is stealing from you and not worth your time.

• No one ever gets fired

A bad coworker can bring everyone down. Maybe others are forced to do their job, or they cause hostility or lack of fluidity in the group. Whatever the case the management team needs to have the backbone to stand up to these people and not let them harm the rest of the group.

• Employees can't tie what they do to the success of the company

Employees need to feel they are part of a bigger project and how their roles are important to the success of the company. The management team needs to keep them informed on company projects and how they are helping and share celebrations with them when goals are met.

2. Your manager - As a leader and a person

Managers set the tone and call the shots for the group and can make your work-life pleasant or crush your spirit. Managers are usually a key component to rather or not a person is happy at work. Good bosses are positive leaders for a department, insightful sources of experience, ambassadors to other departments, and they fight for their team during meetings with upper management.

Bad bosses create a pocket of terror in an otherwise good company and tend to block progress more than help it along.

Here are a few common characteristics of a bad boss: • Everything is top priority

Some managers are very good at creating artificial stress in their department by inflating the urgency of every project. A good manager knows that their employees need a break and save the red alert situations for real emergencies.

• Promising the world to upper management

Weak bosses cannot say no to upper management and pass on every request to their employees even if it is impossible. These bosses rarely provide good leadership. Other departments and even employees in their group take advantage of them. We also see this with managers who are more interested in promoted their own career over the needs of the group they lead. If their employees work long hours to complete every project that is asked it looks good for the manager and cost them little time to say yes.

• Boss is overemotional and egotistic

Many bosses seem to confuse yelling and being a strong leader. Often loss of emotional control is used to hide a manager's lack of real skill. Some schools of management seem to promote harsh words and threats as a way to motivate employees.

• Manipulates situations to take advantage of you

During slow job markets many bosses take advantage of the situation by cutting pay raises to their employees, increasing work hours and generally rolling back

promises made to employees. They know there are not a lot of other jobs available due to economic situations or realities of your type of industry. Bad managers use this to their advantage and forget you are a real person and not a commodity.

• Doesn't give positive feedback or guidance for improvement

Good managers give timely and regular feedback. They frequently and publicly praise employees' work when it is good and give private feedback on how to improve when it needs improvement. Managers should not wait for yearly reviews to state progress or blow up at employees when things have been going downhill for months. Employees should know their role and have expected, required tasks that are achievable. Goals should not be constantly changing. Feedback should be given as goals progress. Finally, if employees work long hours for extended periods of time there needs to be reciprocal signs of appreciation from the management team to make sure the team feels appreciated and rewarded.

• Your boss hates you

A bad boss may not be able to get over perceived differences with you. Maybe they think you have different political beliefs or a different work style than they have. They may allow this to cloud your work relationship and cause them to constantly be negative toward you. Good bosses don't get stuck on these differences and instead can work with a wide array of personality types.

They work well with the entire team and take an interest in each person individually. This allows the boss to know the strengths and weaknesses of each person in the team and know how to motivate them and get the best results from each individual. One person may not work well with constant supervision, but with a little room they may end up being the strongest employee in the team. Building these relationships

also creates camaraderie with the team and can avoid situations where employees appear to lose interest in their work or snap unexpectedly.

• Micromanaging

Bosses who don't trust their employees will spend most of their time (and yours) checking your progress and questioning how you choose to attack a problem. This is fine for new employees or employees who work best if they have constant supervision, but if your manager doesn't recognize your worth and intelligence after 15 years on the job then it can feel demeaning.

This is made even worse if the boss is incompetent and knows less than you do but still insists to look over your shoulder and comment on every action. Managers need to let skilled employees do their job and give them room. They should value their opinions and allow them to bring questions and concerns to the boss when they have them.

• Not around enough

If you boss is never available to be a leader then we have the opposite extreme of micromanagement. Managers are put in place for a purpose and if they do not guide the team, then someone else will. This can cause the members of the team to have to perform the role of the manager without any of the authority. They will not have the connections with upper management and will miss out on the guidance, direction, and experience a good manager would provide. This can cause bickering between group members and force employees to go around the usual chain of command to get things done.

3. Your roll - What do you want to get out your job versus what you are actually getting

Maybe there is nothing inherently wrong with the company, but it is just not the best place for you.

• Not what you expected

If you went into your current position with a salary expectation and you ended up getting paid significantly less, that salary gap is going to eat at you. You may be happy performing a job for free if that is what you set out to do, but if you are not getting paid what you believe you are worth then your salary goals will keep you from being happy at that job.

• You have no interest in what your company does

There is something to be said of being proud of what you do and where you work. If you believe chewing gum is destroying the lives of children then you are not going to be inspired to work harder at a chewing gum factory. If you hate what your company does or are even apathetic to its goals then your only motivation for working there is the money. You will have no enthusiasm and will not care about anything but your paycheck. If the money itself is not so good, then your motivation for the job will be minimal at best.

Alternatively if you believe the products or services your company produces are really great or are helping benefit the world, then you will have extra incentive to go to work every day.

• You work hard, but have no rewards or successes

In a school setting this is called busy work. You work hard each day but nothing of value is ever produced. You never get to celebrate the launch of a new product or start to work on new exciting projects. Every day is the same meaningless

assembly line style tasks. No matter how hard you work there is no difference in your level of success and you never get to see the fruits of your labor.

• You are not doing what you love

You spend a lot of time at work every day. Are you doing what you love or even what you are good at? Is this a creative outlet for your talents and passions or does it just pay the bills.

THINGS YOU MUST CONSIDER BEFORE QUITTING YOUR JOB

If by any chance that one day you wake up asking yourself "Do I really want my job?" then you should start considering the fact that you hate your job and you do not want to stay any longer. Quitting your job however is a long process. A long process of looking onto you financial stability. Can you go on with life along with your family even if you leave your current job? The following statements will help you know what you really want.

Identify real issues and make up your mind:

Hundreds of reasons may affect you desire for your own job. Your employer may not fit your liking, you may not like your job from the start, you hate yourself for not having time for yourself and finally you feel too much pressure from the pile of work loaded on you. Try to point out what you hate about them. And weigh them all if they are enough to make you leave everything.

The first step towards new job:

The next step is to find reasons to change your job. Identify the effects of your job to the aspects of your life. How much time does your job gobble up from your life? Do you by any chance get ideas about your job being too boring and hating it like every day? Does it affect your relationship with your family along with your own health? If your job devours your whole life, then maybe it's time for you to consider leaving it.

Issues you may face:

However, quitting your job faces you to lots of consequences. You need to know your financial stability as of the moment and make plans ahead of time. To know where you can obtain the money needed in the future.

Do your calculations:

First things first, you need to identify the situation. Make a list of where and how to spend your money for each month. And how to earn them. Remember to include your saved money from the past as this can supplement you through your money needs in the future.

HOW YOU SHOULD RESIGN FROM YOUR JOB

Resigning from your current job depends on the scenario that you are currently facing. Most of the time candidates resign from their jobs to join a better opportunity. A lot of people resign because they had enough of the job and can't work there anymore. Resigning in a dignified way is what every employee wants and some people are not lucky enough to leave a company without burning bridges. Suppose you want to leave your job and have no idea how to do it. Follow these guidelines and you will be able to leave one a good note:

• € First of all check your contract. What does it say about leaving? Some companies have rules that require the employees to serve a notice period before formally quitting their jobs. If you have that clause in your contract then serve that notice in an email addressed to the higher management, CEO and the HR department.

• € Don't go around telling every one of your colleagues that you want to leave. Not everyone in the company is your friend. Just tell the higher management or your team leader or a senior colleague that you have finally decided to leave the company. Do not tell everyone before you get a green signal from the higher management. And it is better if you disclose this one week before you leave.

• € What is your reason for leaving? A lot of people are going to ask about this and the best answer is that you found a better opportunity that you couldn't refuse. Do not in any case tell people any other reason, no matter how much

you hate working there, do not let anyone know that you are leaving simply because you had enough.

• € Some companies may have an exit interview with you. This is usually not a standard procedure but usually this interview involves the higher management or the HR asking you why you are leaving. Stick to the answer stated above. There is no need to let them know what's wrong with the company. Do not turn this into a consulting session and stick to the corporate answer. If there is nothing nice you can say, then just keep quiet and walk out of there.

• € Your resignation letter is probably the most important thing right now. What do you want to say in it? This is entirely up to you. If you enjoyed your work, then write a thankful email to your colleagues and the management. If you are glad to leave and had enough, then a quick resignation will be enough. A couple of lines about the reason and the date when you plan to leave will be enough. You can also ask the HR or the CEO to spread the word of you leaving the company or you can email your colleagues yourself later on before you leave.

TIPS FOR QUITTING YOUR JOB THE BEST WAY POSSIBLE

Give At Least 2 Weeks Notice

For most jobs, the standard two weeks' notice will work. However, there are some instances in which you might want to provide more notice. For example, I was a store manager at a discount retailer. I knew my replacement would need to attend a 30 day training course before becoming the replacement manager.

For that reason, I provided a 45 day notice. There are some situations in which too much notice can backfire on you (you want to quit, so do it now), but if you play your cards right, giving the proper amount of notice for quitting your job will work in your favor.

Do a Verbal and Written Notice

You should also hand in a written and typed letter of resignation when quitting your job. However, there are benefits to delivering that letter in person and having a private conversation when doing so. This gives the impression that you cared about your job, the company, and the time spent there. You basically show that you aren't another employee who is just interested in heading for greener pastures. Managers, especially in smaller companies where they will remember you, like this approach.

Don't Provide Too Much Information

When writing your letter of resignation and when speaking with your supervisor verbally, it is important that you provide the basics and that is it. It is also important for you to provide the information that is the least harmful to your future.

For example, say you are quitting your job because you can't stand a coworker. This is a good reason personally to quit, but a bad one to tell your supervisor. Do not go into too much detail about anything bad related to your job

or the company. State you are relocating, looking for a new challenge, and so forth. Keep it short, simple, and sweet.

Offer to Help Train Replacement

This is another offer that you might not get taken up on, but you have nothing to lose by stating that you would be willing to help train your replacement. This is another way to show that you are not up and leaving for greener pastures without a care in the world. It is one of those statements that can help land you a good reference from your current employer. If your employer does take you up on your offer to train your replacement, do so wisely and carefully. Remember to follow all company rules and guidelines. Also, remember to never talk bad or down about the company, the job, the supervisors, or the coworkers.

Don't Burn Any Bridges You May Need to Later Cross

Many times, hardworking Americans quit their jobs because they came across a better job opportunity. However, a good percentage of employees are leaving because they feel underappreciated and undervalued at work. You might feel as if your boss is a big jerk who should go back to kindergarten again to learn how to be polite. No matter how much you have the urge to tell your supervisor or coworkers to go and shove it, don't! You never want to burn any bridges you might need to cross later. After all, your coworkers and or bosses might switch jobs in the future as well. Basically, you never know when you'll come across them again.

REASONS YOU SHOULD PROVIDE TWO WEEKS NOTICE

Reason 1: It Is Expected

Somewhere along the line, it became the standard rule of thumb that you should always provide your current employer with at least two weeks notice when you want to quit your job.

No one is really sure when this unwritten rule became official or how, but it is what most companies expect. In fact, you'll find it written in many employment contracts that two weeks of written and verbal notice must be provided.

Reason 2: Enough Time to Find a Replacement

Most workers perform a task that must be refilled by another or a new employee. Even if you are simply a cashier at your local Walmart, your position will likely be filled once you quit your job. Employees who quit their jobs on a whim and without notice impact many. That company must then scatter to fill all slots of a schedule. By providing two weeks' notice, you provide your employer with accurate and ample time to find and possibly begin to train your replacement.

Reason 3: It Helps You Secure a Good Reference

As previously stated, two weeks' notice when looking to quit your job has become the standard. Moreover, that two weeks will give your current employer ample time to find a replacement for you. What does this all lead to?

It leads to you likely receiving a good reference. In fact, it is common for even the best performing employees who receive a bad reference after quitting on a whim and without providing notice. So let's say that you worked at Company A for 5 years and did a

great job, are you ready to toss all that hard work down the tube because you didn't want to put in two more weeks worth of work?

RESIGNING WITH DIGNITY AND STYLE

There are right ways and wrong to resign from your job. Doing it the wrong way can lead to bad feelings between you and your employer recriminations or even a bad reference. On the other hand, resigning the right way will contribute to continued success in both your personal and professional development.

Make sure you know what you are doing, be positive and prepared. Before making up your mind consider the options carefully. Are you committed to leaving? Make a list of reasons why you really should resign.

What procedure should you follow to tender your resignation? If an employee plans to resign from his service then, he/she should submit Employment Resignation Letter to the HR manager or employer, showing his/her intention to terminate his/her service in the company or organization.

There are various reasons, which prompts an employee to resign from his job and they include, better job opportunity in another organization, working environment, moving out of the city or country, poor pay scale and family commitments. Informing verbally, about his service termination is not proper corporate tradition to inform the employer. These reasons make it necessary, to follow right corporate culture and, tender his written resignation, according to the company rules and regulations. He should also cite job quitting reasons in the letter.

It is also necessary for the employee to understand that, leaving the job is not an easy task and lots of explanations are to be tendered for terminating his service in the company.

Again, the employer may want employee to continue, because of the over workloads in the company, which needs his active participation or it may not be possible to get another efficient personnel for the same position in the short period of time. Such reasons make it essential to handle resignation issue,

delicately and carefully for maintaining cordial relation with the employer in future and, to avoid any legal tangles or breach of contract.

It is also advisable that, a worker, intending to quit his job must follow proper resignation channel. Many companies have, their own job termination clauses, which are agreed by the employee, at the time of hiring. These terms and conditions may include, serving advance job quitting information, confidentiality provision, pre quit notice and resignation letter.

If company procedures are not followed by the employee and, if there is any breach of contract then, he may have to face numerous legal complications, which may spoil his relation with the employer or may be detrimental to his future career prospects.

WHAT TO DO AFTER QUITTING YOUR DAY JOB

There are many people who choose to make their money online operating an online business. Working online in the comfort of your own home is a dream for most people. Working at home is not that hard to do if you find the right online business. Making extra money online is something that we all can do if we know where to start and how to go about doing it. First, you must find an online business that is of interest to you. Then you should set some goals and work toward them to operate a successful business at home. Do some research and find out how other people are making a living online and the methods in which they use.

You will find out by researching that there are many business opportunities that you can start by using your home computer with little or no money upfront. Once your business is up and running and you know that you are doing well you should be able to quit your day job and spend all your time working from home.

When working from home your must find a business that you take a lot of interest in doing. You will need to find something that you will want to stick with over time and one that you will not tire of quickly. With all the online business opportunities available, you should be able to find the right business for you to make a living from home. Discovering what you are good at can make choosing the right online business easier. You may be good at typing or selling products and want to use your talents to start a successful online business. Quitting your day job may not be as far away as you think once your new work from home business becomes successful.

Becoming our own boss is a dream that we have all had at one point in our lives. You need to take the proper action and set goals for yourself to make this happen. Just because you are at your home, you must still treat your work as a regular job and not get distracted with other things that go on inside your home. Putting in the right amount of work each day is very important to make your business grow and become successful.

Researching jobs online and finding out how people operate their own online businesses can give you pointers for operating your own online business. Pushing yourself each day and doing as much work as you can, can also help with your success.

GETTING TO YOUR DREAM JOB

Your work place is getting boring and you have a boss not quite from hell, but close. Your co-workers are ready and waiting to stab you in the back to get ahead. You know this is not where you want to be, so why stick with it? Are you ready for the challenge that will truly get you your dream job? Many are, and it's not the most difficult thing to do.

Life isn't about a routine of day in, day out in some job you didn't really want. It's awful to feel stuck, when you realize you've still got the rest of your working life to come. Life is about living and feeling alive, so make some changes and realize your full potential! No one is forcing you to stay in a job you hate and no one is holding you back from your dreams - except yourself, that is.

And the fact, the honest truth that it's all down to you is often the bitterest pill to swallow.

So, what do you really enjoy in life. Is it a hobby or a passion? Whatever it is you love doing is a huge hint! Have you ever thought of turning that hobby into a dream job that you'll look forward to every day? You could turn your hobby into a real, exciting, successful job with a little determination and some close attention.

That's right - it's all about focus. Decide what it is you'd rather be doing, and then find out all you can about how you need to get there. Do your homework on whether you need credentials or qualifications to turn your hobby into employment. Find out the steps you need to make that will bring you to where you want to be and lay down a plan.

Remember, you're not going to get anywhere over night. Miracles don't happen and hard work, effort, and the right choices to move you forward will have amazing results. If you need training, part time courses or night school can let you keep

your day job and work towards a new career in your spare time. Hey, you might even find them in your current workplace, so you can get them for free

Volunteer. Network. Apprentice under someone who excels at what you want to do. Offering free services in exchange for the learning experience can be a great way to break into a new industry or career. Talk to everyone you know about your plans; the more contacts and support you have, the more it will help you stay focused on your goals and provide opportunities.

Don't give up. Making life changes takes time and isn't always easy. You may face some stumbling blocks along the way to a dream job. If you remember your goals and you've taken the time to lay down your steps and plans, you'll be better prepared to find a way around the obstacle.

Obstacles are valuable opportunities for lessons in achieving what you want. Be prepared to face them and accept the challenge of resolving them. You'll also gain plenty of wisdom and experience while you work towards securing your dream job and a life of happiness and satisfaction.

If you truly believe you can, with no 'glass ceilings' to hold you back you'll release potential and show the world what you can do. You are the only person in charge of your life.

GETTING THE MOST OUT OF YOUR NEW JOB

The business arena is constantly changing with new markets and ways of doing business regularly emerging. We spend a large proportion of our time and our lives at work. With work related stress being a major cause of ill-health and unhappiness let us look at how to take better care of ourselves and how to take better control of our situations. There are several golden rules that can make life easier for everyone.

• Be flexible.

Be aware that a work description is merely a guide to your required skills sets. If you have an opportunity to do something outside of your ability, try to treat it as an opportunity to grow and evolve new skills and abilities rather than as a cause of work related stress.

You can look for appropriate training but treat it as a positive opportunity. This attitude could make your working more interesting and enable you to become more competent in several other areas.

• Smile. Being happy is contagious.

If you smile and look happy people around you will usually respond well. You will get a better reaction from the people you deal with. Smiling is not the same as being the joker and wasting time. It is about being pleasant, good natured and approachable. Looking as if you are happy to be there, doing your job.

• Be enthusiastic.

This helps you find more energy and satisfaction from the things that you do. It keeps your attitude and mindset positive and willing. Do your tasks with commitment and enthusiasm and you will find satisfaction and fulfillment from

them, from filing papers to driving miles to the next meeting. Appreciate the opportunity to grow and do each task well. Be proud of your work.

• Be positive.

Avoid negative people and attitudes. There is often more than one way of looking at something. Be aware of the potential for different points of view. Keep yourself in a receptive frame of mind. Negativity breeds negativity and is a major cause of work related stress. Work on surrounding yourself with positive thoughts and positive people. Be too busy for the negative ones.

CONCLUSION

Are you sick and tired of feeling stuck in that hell of a job? Have you had enough of having your greatness held hostage for so long? Don't you think it's time you got out of your rut and back into your groove?

It's time for you to get out of the darkness and step back into the light, it's time to stop procrastinating and worrying, and it's time to take action and to get your life back on track.

Anyone can encourage you, anyone can give you the tools so that you can help yourself, and take your life to any level that you want. However, no one will do the work for you, you are the master of your fate, you are the captain of your soul.

You are the only person that can take the actions that are required to get you out of that job that is reducing the quality of your life and back into your groove, only you can get out of the darkness and step back into the light, no one can do it for you, and to be honest, you shouldn't want anyone to do it for you.

You are the one that got yourself into this predicament, and you sure as hell are the only person that can get you out of it.

Make a decision today to get out of that hell of a job and step back into the light, make a decision to get out of your rut and get back into your groove. Take action, followed by more action, backed up with sheer determination and you will step back into the light, break free from the self-imposed limitations that have been keeping you stuck in a rut for so long and get back into your groove.

Take action today, even if it's the smallest step, as long as it's a step in the right direction, that's all that matters, tiny steps, take focused daily action towards achieving your goals and before you know it you will be totally stunned at how far you have come in such a short period of time.

Stop procrastinating and worrying about what might or might not go right, and take action, design an action plan and take daily action on that plan and you will literally astound yourself.

It's time for you to stop playing small, and to start playing big, make a decision to stop settling for the scraps from the table of life. Get out of the darkness and step back into the light.